This book belongs to:

About Ysolda

Ysolda Teague is a young Scottish designer who has published popular designs in Twist Collective and knitty. Her many other patterns are available on her website and blog, ysolda.com. She lives and works in Edinburgh but loves to travel, especially when it means meeting the people who make her patterns.

Thank you!

to Sheena Stewart, Struan Teague, Shawn Teague, Hannah Haworth, Laura Chau, Sarah Stanfield, Kate Davies, Rebecca Redston and Kate Blecich for all of your help in putting together this collection.

And thank you to all of the knitters who have read my blog, purchased my patterns and encouraged my designing, this wouldn't exist without your support.

Published by Ysolda Teague © Ysolda Teague 2009

Whimsical Little Knits

by Golda

Abbreviations

k - knit

p - purl

st(s) - stitch(es)

st st - stockinette / stocking st

bind off - also known as cast off

sl - slip

pm - place marker

slm - slip marker

yo - yarn over

k2tog - knit 2 together

ssk - slip, slip, knit slipped sts together

p2tog - purl 2 together

sl1, k2tog, psso - slip 1, k2tog, lift sl st over st just worked

m1 - make one (pick up the strand between the needles from the front and place on the left needle tip, knit it through the back loop)

kfb - knit in front and back of next st

beg - begin(ning)

rnd(s) - round(s)

rep(s) - repeat(s)

rem - remaining

dpn(s) - double pointed needle(s)

RS - right side

WS - wrong side

MC - main colour

CC - contrast colour

Confused?

If you're not sure how to do something or are confused by an instruction have a look at the support page on my website which has links to many useful tutorials and answers to frequently asked questions.
http://ysolda.com/support/
If that doesn't help you can email me at support@ysolda.com

Ishbel

Ishbel is a simple shawl pattern that can be worked in two sizes and two different yarn weights. The smaller, fingering weight version makes a cosy but pretty scarf while the larger, lace weight version can be worn as a scarf or draped elegantly around the shoulders. The solid stockinette centre lends simplicity to the design and adds extra warmth when knitted in thicker yarn. Ishbel is edged with a beautiful vine pattern and finished with elegant scalloped points.

The shawl begins at the centre and is worked outwards to the edging. Working increases at both ends of every row, rather than every second, creates a relatively shallow triangular shawl that makes it the perfect shape to wear as a scarf. Either size can of course be worked in either yarn weight.

Materials

Yarn - 330 yds / 300m [610 yds / 555m] lace or fingering (4ply) weight yarn. Smaller blue shawl shown in Old Maiden Aunt Alpaca Merino 4ply (50% suri alpaca / 50% merino, 330 yds / 300m, 3.53oz /100g) in Moody.
Larger pink shawl shown in Fyberspates Laceweight Scrumptious (45% silk / 55% merino, 1095 yds / 1000m, 3.53oz / 100g) in Kisses.
Needles - 4mm circular needle (24" / 60cm or longer)

Gauge

20 sts and 30 rows = 4" / 10cm in st st. Matching exact gauge isn't crucial, but your gauge will obviously affect the finished size.

Sizes

Directions for 2 sizes are given - s[l], approx 48.5[66]" / 123[168]cm wide and 14.5[19.5]" / 37[49.5]cm long at centre.

Directions

Cast on 3 sts; knit 6 rows. Pick up and k 3 sts from vertical edge of garter stitch, then 3 sts from cast on edge. 9 sts.

Stocking stitch centre

Row 1 (WS): k3, yo, p to 3 sts from end, yo, k3. 11 sts.

Row 2: k3, yo, k2, yo, k1 (this st will be referred to as the centre st from now on and can be marked with a safety pin if desired), yo, k2, yo, k3. 15 sts.

Row 3: Repeat row 1. 17 sts.

Row 4: k 3, yo, k to centre st, yo, k1, yo, k to 3 sts from end, yo, k3. 21 sts. Rep rows 3 and 4 25[33] more times. 171[219] sts.

Repeat row 1 once more. 173[221] sts.

Vine pattern

Using either charts or written directions work section A - 197[245] sts; then work B - 221[269] sts. L size only work A and B again - 317 sts. Both sizes work A once more - 245[341] sts; then C - 261[357]sts.

Section A - written directions

Row 1: k3, yo, k1, k2tog, *k3, (yo, k1) twice, sl1, k2tog, psso, rep from * to 8 sts before centre stitch, k3, (yo, k1) twice, ssk, (k1, yo) twice, k1, k2tog, (k1, yo) twice, k3, *sl1, k2tog, psso, (k1, yo) twice, k3, rep from * to 6 sts from end, ssk, k1, yo, k3.

Row 2 and all following even rows: k3, yo, p to 3 sts from end, yo, k3.

Row 3: k3, yo, k2, yo, sl1, k2tog, psso, * k2, yo, k3, yo, sl1, k2tog, psso, rep from * to 9 sts before centre stitch, k2, yo, k3, yo, ssk, k2, yo, k1, yo, k2, k2tog, yo, k3, yo, k2, *sl1, k2tog, psso, yo, k3, yo, k2, rep from * to 8 sts from end, sl1, k2tog, psso, yo, k2, yo, k3.

Row 5: k3, yo, k1, yo, k3, sl1, k2tog, psso, *(k1, yo) twice, k3, sl1, k2tog, psso, rep from * to 10 sts before centre stitch, (k1, yo) twice, k3, ssk, k3, yo, k1, yo, k3, k2tog, k3, (yo, k1) twice, *sl1, k2tog, psso, k3, (yo, k1) twice, rep from * to 10 sts from end, sl1, k2tog, psso, k3, yo, k1, yo, k3.

Row 7: k3, yo, k4, yo, k2, sl1, k2tog, psso, *yo, k3, yo, k2, sl1, k2tog, psso, rep from * to 11 sts before centre stitch, yo, k3, yo, k2, ssk, k4, yo, k1, yo, k4, k2tog, k2, yo, k3, yo, *sl1, k2tog, psso, k2, yo, k3, yo, rep from * to 12 sts from end, sl1, k2tog, psso, k2, yo, k4, yo, k3.

Row 8: rep row 2.

Section B - written directions

Row 1: k3, yo, k1, k2tog, *k3, (yo, k1) twice, sl1, k2tog, psso, rep from * to 4 sts before centre st, k3, (yo, k1) 3 times, yo, k3 *sl1, k2tog, psso, (k1, yo) twice, k3, rep from * to 6 sts from end, ssk, k1, yo, k3.

Row 2 and all following even rows: k3, yo, p to 3 sts from end, yo, k3.

Row 3: k3, yo, k2, yo, sl1, k2tog, psso, * k2, yo, k3, yo, sl1, k2tog, psso, rep from * to 5 sts before centre stitch, k2, yo, k3, yo, k1, yo, k3, yo, k2, *sl1, k2tog, psso, yo, k3, yo, k2, rep from * to 8 sts from end, sl1, k2tog, psso, yo, k2, yo, k3.

Row 5: k3, yo, k1, yo, k3, sl1, k2tog, psso, *(k1, yo) twice, k3, sl1, k2tog, psso, rep from * to 6 sts before centre stitch, k1, yo, k5, yo, k1, yo, k5, yo, k1, *sl1, k2tog, psso, k3, (yo, k1) twice, rep from * to 10 sts from end, sl1, k2tog, psso, k3, yo, k1, yo, k3.

Row 7: k3, yo, k4, yo, k2, sl1, k2tog, psso, *yo, k3, yo, k2, sl1, k2tog, psso, rep from * to 7 sts before centre stitch, yo, k7, yo, k1, yo, k7, yo, *sl1, k2tog, psso, k2, yo, k3, yo, rep from * to 12 sts from end, sl1, k2tog, psso, k2, yo, k4, yo, k3.

Row 8: rep row 2.

Section C - written directions

Row 1: k3, yo, k1, k2tog, *k3, (yo, k1) twice, sl1, k2tog, psso, rep from * to 4 sts before centre st, k3, (yo, k1) 3 times, yo, k3 *sl1, k2tog, psso, (k1, yo) twice, k3, rep from * 6 sts from end, ssk, k1, yo, k3.

Row 2 and all following even rows: k3, yo, p to 3 sts from end, yo, k3.

Row 3: k3, yo, k2, yo, sl1, k2tog, psso, * k2, yo, k3, yo, sl1, k2tog, psso, rep from * to 5 sts before centre stitch, k2, yo, k3, yo, k1, yo, k3, yo, k2, *sl1, k2tog, psso, yo, k3, yo, k2, rep from * to 8 sts from end, sl1, k2tog, psso, yo, k2, yo, k3.

Row 5: k3, yo, k1, yo, k3, sl1, k2tog, psso, *(k1, yo) twice, k3, sl1, k2tog, psso, rep from * to 6 sts before centre stitch, k3, yo, k7, yo, k3, *sl1, k2tog, psso, k3, (yo, k1) twice, rep from * to 10 sts from end, sl1, k2tog, psso, k3, yo, k1, yo, k3.

Row 6: rep row 2.

Edging

Using either charts or written directions work section D - 277[373] sts; then work E - 345[465] sts.

Section D - written directions

Row 1: k3, yo, k3, *k1, yo, k2, sl1, k2tog, psso, k2, yo, rep from * to 7 sts from end, k4, yo, k3.

Row 2 and all following even rows: k3, yo, p to 3 sts from end, yo, k3.

Row 3: k3, yo, k1, k2tog, k2, yo, *k1, yo, k2, sl1, k2tog, psso, k2, yo, rep from * to 9 sts from end, k1, yo, k2, ssk, k1, yo, k3.

Row 5: k3, yo, k3, k2tog, k2, yo, *k1, yo, k2, sl1, k2tog, psso, k2, yo, rep from * to 11 sts from end, k1, yo, k2, ssk, k3, yo, k3.

Row 7: k3, yo, k2, yo, k2, sl1, k2tog, psso, k2, yo, *k1, yo, k2, sl1, k2tog, psso, k2, yo, rep from * to 13 sts from end, k1, yo, k2, sl1, k2tog, psso, k2, yo, k2, yo, k3.

Row 8: rep row 2.

Section E - written directions

Row 1: k3, yo, k3, *k1, yo, k7, yo, rep from * to 7 sts from end, k4, yo, k3.

Finishing

With WS facing bind off loosely:
*p2 tog, sl st on right needle back to left needle, rep from * to end. Weave in ends. Wet block, pinning top edge straight and pinning out eyelets along bottom edge into points.

Ishbel Charts Work section A - 197[245] sts; then work B - 221[269] sts. L size only work A and B again - 317 sts. Both sizes work A once more - 245[341] sts; then work C - 261[357] sts; then work D - 277[373] sts. Edging; work section E - 345[465] sts.

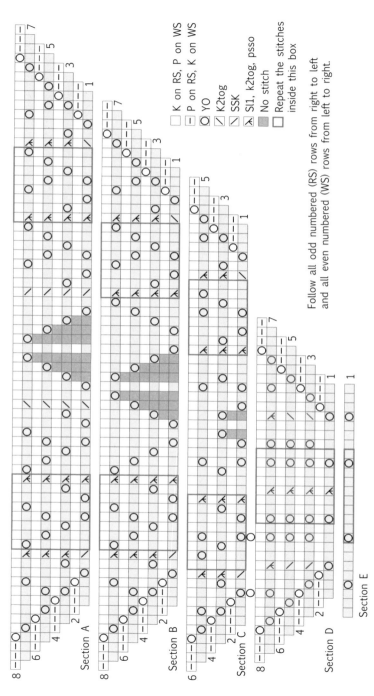

Section A

Section B

Section C

Section D

Section E

K on RS, P on WS
- P on RS, K on WS
O YO
/ K2tog
\ SSK
⅄ Sl1, k2tog, psso
▨ No stitch
□ Repeat the stitches inside this box

Follow all odd numbered (RS) rows from right to left and all even numbered (WS) rows from left to right.

Ishbel Beret

My friend Rebecca had yarn leftover from her Ishbel and wanted a beret pattern that would go with the scarf. So this one's for you Rebecca.

Materials

Yarn - 155[175, 195, 215] yds / 140[160, 180, 200]m lace or fingering / 4ply weight yarn. Shown in Handmaiden Casbah (81% Merino, 9% Cashmere,10% Nylon; 355 yds / 325m; 4oz / 115g) in Stone.

Needles - 3mm 16" / 40 cm circular, 4mm 16" / 40 cm circular, 4mm dpns

Notions - scrap yarn for provisional cast on, marker.

Gauge

20sts and 30 rows = 4"/10cm in st st with larger needle.

Sizes

xs[s, m, l] to fit approx head circumference of 18[20, 22, 24]" / 46[51, 56, 61] cm

Band

With smaller needle provisionally cast on 84[96, 108, 120] sts. Join rnd, placing marker to mark beg of rnd. K 10 rnds; p 1 rnd; k 9 rnds.

Switch to larger needle and k 1 rnd. Undo provisional cast on and slip held sts onto smaller needle. Hold smaller needle behind larger. Using right tip of larger needle *k working st tog with cast on st, rep from * to end. 84[96, 108, 120] sts. The rest of the hat will be worked with the larger size.

Vine Pattern

Note: At the end of rnd 7 stop 1 st from end and re-position marker to mark this point as the beg of the rnd. After completing rnd 10 k1 and re-position marker to mark this point as the beg of the rnd.

Rnd 1 and all following odd rnds: k even.

Using either chart or written directions work rnd 2 once then rnds 3-10 2[2, 3, 3] times then rnds 3-8 once more. For a less slouchy hat work one less rep of rnds 3-10.

Rnd 2: (yo, k3) to end. 112[128, 144, 160] sts.

Rnd 4: (k1, yo, k1, sl1, k2tog, psso, k3, yo) to end.

Rnd 6: (k2, yo, sl1, k2tog, psso, k2, yo, k1) to end.
Rnd 8: (yo, k3, sl1, k2tog, psso, k1, yo, k1) to end.
Rnd 10: (k1, yo, k2, sl1, k2tog, psso, yo, k2) to end.

Vine pattern - chart

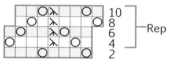

Follow every row on chart from right to left.

Crown

When sts no longer comfortably fit around circular switch to dpns, distributing sts evenly.
Rnd 1 and all following odd rnds other than those written out or charted: k even.

Crown - written directions
Rnds 2, 4, 6, 8: (k1, yo, k2, sl1, k2tog, psso, k2, yo) to end.
Rnd 9: (k3, sl1, k2tog, psso, k2) to end. 84[96, 108, 120] sts.
Rnds 10, 12, 14, 16: (k1, yo, k1, sl1, k2tog, psso, k1, yo) to end.
Rnd 17: (k2, sl1, k2tog, psso, k1) to end. 56[64, 72, 80] sts.
Rnds 18, 20, 22, 24: (k1, yo, sl1, k2tog, psso, yo) to end.

Crown - chart

		18, 20, 22, 24
		17
		10, 12, 14, 16
		9
		2, 4, 6, 8

Top
Rnd 1: k.
Rnd 2: k2tog to end. 28[32, 36, 40] sts.
Rep last 2 rnds twice. 7[8, 9, 10] sts.

Finishing
Break yarn and draw through rem sts, pulling up tightly. Weave in ends. Block over a disc shaped object such as a plate.

Mousie

A sweet little mouse that's fun to knit from just a small amount of yarn. Mousie's knit almost entirely in the round with minimal seaming.

The body is worked in one piece, beginning with the charming I-cord tail and ending with the tip of his nose. Then sts are picked up for the simple I-cord limbs and big, alert ears. Mousie is the perfect gift for anyone who needs a mischievous little companion, including yourself.

Materials

Yarn - 55 yds / 50m for MC and 11 yds / 10m for CC of fingering (4ply), sport or double knitting weight yarn. Shown in Jaeger Matchmaker Merino 4ply in Graphite and Araucania Ranco Sock in 492

Needles - 2mm set of 4 dpns if using fingering (4ply) weight yarn or 3mm dpns if using sport or double knitting weight yarn.
Notions - scrap of black yarn for embroidering eyes, toy stuffing.

Gauge

Exact gauge isn't important - you can use any yarn with needles a couple of sizes smaller than recommended to give a tight fabric that the stuffing won't poke through.

Size will vary depending on your gauge, but my fingering weight mouse measures approx. 3.5" / 9cm from bottom to the tip of his inquisitive nose.

Tail

With CC cast on 3 sts. Work I-cord: *k3, slide sts to other end of dpn without turning, rep from * until tail measures desired length. Switch to MC and work 2 more rows of I cord. Without turning work next row: kfb in each st. 6 sts.

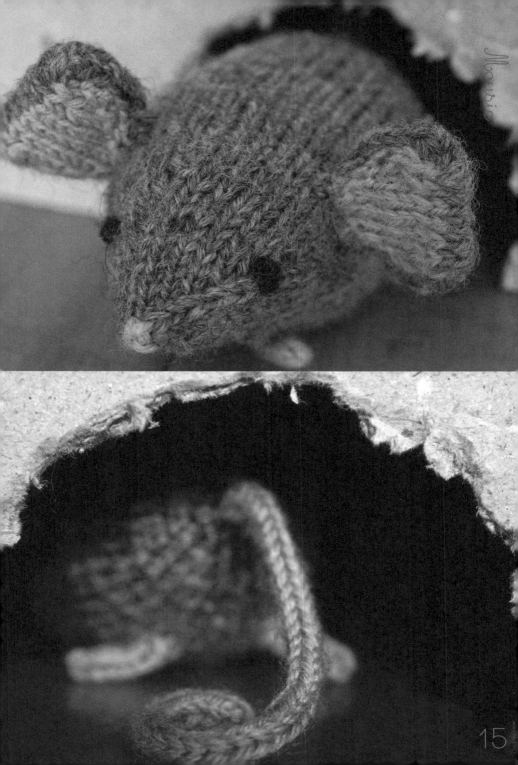

Body

Stuff the body with small amounts of stuffing as you go. Arrange sts so that there are 2 on each of 3 needles and join rnd.

Rnd 1 and all following odd rnds: k.

Rnd 2: kfb in each st. 12 sts.

Rnd 4: (k1, kfb) to end. 18 sts.

Rnd 6: (k2, kfb) to end. 24 sts.

Rnd 8: (k3, kfb) to end. 30 sts.

Rnd 10: (k4, kfb) to end. 36 sts.

Rnd 11: k.

Rnd 12: k4, m1, k to 4 sts from end of rnd, m1, k4. 38 sts.

Rnd 13-16: rep rnds 11 and 12 twice. 42 sts.

Rnd 17-27: k 11 rnds.

Rnd 28: k3, ssk, k to 5 sts from end of rnd, k2tog, k3. 40 sts.

Rnd 29: k.

Rnd 30-37: rep 28-29 4 times. 32 sts.

Rnd 38: (k6, k2tog) to end. 28 sts.

Rnd 40: (k5, k2tog) to end. 24 sts.

Rnd 42: (k4, k2tog) to end. 20 sts.

Rnd 44: (k3, k2tog) to end. 16 sts.

Rnd 46: (k2, k2tog) to end. 12 sts.

> **Tip** - for a toy that won't be played with by an infant or small child you can stuff the bottom with dried pulses or plastic beads to weight it.

Rnd 48: (k1, k2tog) to end. 8 sts.

Rnd 49: switch to CC, (k2tog) to end. 4 sts.

Break yarn and draw through remaining 4 sts, fasten tightly and hide tail on inside.

Feet

With head pointing towards you pick up and knit 3 sts with CC for front paw, as shown in diagram (rounder side is the belly) and work 4 rows in I cord. Break yarn and thread through sts, fasten tightly and hide tail on inside. Repeat for 2nd front paw. Work back paws in the same way picking up and knitting 4 sts and working 6 rows in I cord.

Ears

Work ears back and forth on 2 needles. With CC and head towards you pick up and knit 4 sts in position shown in diagram.

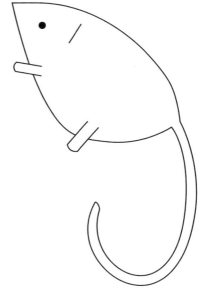

Row 1 and all following odd rows: p.
Row 2: k1, m1, k2, m1, k1. 6 sts.
Row 4: k1, m1, k4, m1, k1. 8 sts.
Row 6: k1, m1, k6, m1, k1. 10 sts.
Row 8: k.
Row 10: k1, ssk, k4, k2tog, k1. 8 sts.
Row 11: switch to MC, p.
Row 12: k1, m1, k6, m1, k1. 10 sts.
Row 14: k1, m1, k8, m1, k1. 12 sts.
Row 15-21: work even in st st.
Row 22: k1, k2tog, k6, k2tog, k1. 10 sts.
Row 23: p1, p2tog, p4, p2tog, p1. 8 sts.
Row 24: k1, k2tog, k2, k2tog, k1. 6 sts.

Finishing

Bind off. Use tail to sew sides of ear together and bound off edge to head. Rep for 2nd ear.
Hide all loose yarn tails on inside. Embroider french knot eyes with black yarn.

17

Tiny Shoes

Adorable Mary Jane style booties worked in fingering weight yarn. The perfect way to use up your leftover sock yarn and showcase two special little buttons. These tiny shoes are a wonderfully quick but satisfying knit that's sure to be an appreciated gift.

Materials

Yarn - 44[55, 66] yds / 40[50, 60] m of fingering (4ply) weight yarn. Shown in Handmaiden Casbah (81% Merino, 9% Cashmere, 10% Nylon; 355 yds / 325m; 4oz / 115g) in Stone. If you wish to knit a swatch this will require more yarn.
Needles - 3mm set of 4 dpns.
Notions - 2 small buttons.

Sizes

s[m, l] - to fit approx foot length of 3[3.5, 4]" / 7.5[8.75, 10]cm
Babies grow fast so if in doubt make a larger size, and don't worry too much about getting the exact gauge - they'll fit soon enough!

Gauge

28 sts and 36 rows = 4" / 10cm in st st.

Strap

With 2 dpns cast on 5 sts and work in I cord: *k5, slide sts to other end of dpn without turning, rep from *; for 36[40, 44] rows.
Bind off 2 sts. Continue working in I cord on rem 3 sts for 10 more rows, bind off.

Upper

Left shoe -
Beginning at cast on end of strap pick up and knit 18[20, 22] sts from strands of yarn across back of I cord. Cast on 18[20, 22] sts next to last picked up st.

Right shoe -
Cast on 18[20, 22] sts, beginning at cast on end of strap pick up and purl 18[20, 22] sts next to last cast on st from strands of yarn across back of I cord. Turn, k 1 row.

Both shoes - distribute sts on 3 dpns and join rnd. K 10, this will be the beg of the rnd. 36[40, 44] sts.

Arrange sts so that the next18[20, 22] sts are on needle 1 and there are 9[10, 11] sts on needles 2 and 3.

Left shoe only - k 1 rnd.

Both shoes -
Next rnd: k to 6[7,8] sts before the end of needle 1, (yo, k1) 12[14, 16] times (needle 2 should begin with a yo), k to end. 48[54, 60] sts: 24[27,

30] sts on needle 1, 15[17, 19] sts on needle 2 and 9[10, 11] sts on needle 3.

K 8 rnds.

Sole

Beg with a p rnd work 5 rnds in garter st: p 1 rnd, k 1 rnd.

Size 1 only -
Next rnd: k4, k2tog, k to 6 sts from end of needle 1, k2tog, k8, k2tog, k to 6 sts from end of rnd, k2tog, k4. 56 sts.
Next rnd: p.

Size m and l only -
Next rnd: k3, k2tog, k to 5 sts from end of needle 1, k2tog, k6, k2tog, k to 5 sts from end of rnd, k2tog, k3. 50[52] sts.
Next rnd: p.

All sizes -
Next rnd: k2, k2tog, k to 4 sts from end of needle 1, k2tog, k4, k2tog, k to 4 sts from end of rnd, k2tog, k2. 44[46, 48] sts.
Next rnd: p.
Next rnd: k1, k2tog, k to 3 sts from end of needle 1, k2tog, k2, k2tog, k to 3 sts from end of rnd, k2tog, k1. 40[42, 44] sts.

Next rnd: p.
Next rnd: k2tog, k to 2 sts from end of needle 1, k2tog twice, k to 2 sts from end of rnd, k2tog. 36[38, 40] sts.
Next rnd: p.

Finishing
Slip sts on needle 3 onto needle 2. Kitchener stitch the 2 sets of stitches on needles 1 and 2 together. Sew narrow section of strap into a loop, joining the 2 bound off edges. Sew button securely to cast on end of strap.

Poppy

Meet Poppy, a sweet little doll who would make the perfect gift for any child. Or, if you can't bear to give her away, she'd love to be friends with you too. Knit seamlessly in the round from the top down Poppy is quick to knit from small amounts of yarn. Instructions are given for her cute Mary Janes and dress, but dressing her is a great opportunity to get creative.

Materials

Yarn - Body: 130 yds / 120m of double knitting weight yarn. Shown in Rowan Purelife Organic Wool (100% wool, 137yds / 126m, 1.76oz / 50g) in Natural.

Dress, shoes and barrettes: 77 yds / 70m of double knitting weight yarn. Shown in Rowan Pure Wool DK (100% wool, 136yds / 124m, 1.76oz / 50g) in Kiss.

Hair: 65 yds / 60m of double knitting weight yarn. Shown in Rowan Pure Wool DK in Mocha.

Needles - 3mm dpns or circulars for your preferred method of knitting small circumferences in the round.

Notions - toy stuffing, 2 small buttons approx .5" / 12mm in diameter, stitch markers, scrap cardboard.

Gauge 26 sts = 4" / 10cm in st st. Exact gauge isn't too important and the size of the doll can be varied by using yarn in different weights. The important thing is to work at a reasonably tight gauge so the stuffing can't poke through.

Size approx 12" / 30cm from the tip of her toes to the top of her head.

Head

With body yarn cast on 24 sts, 12 sts on each of 2 needle tips of circular **or** 12 sts on 1 and 6 sts on each of 2 dpns, using either Judy's Magic Cast On or a figure of 8 cast on. The 2 sections of 12 sts will be referred to as the front and back sts from now on.

Add small amounts of stuffing as you go, stuffing neck firmly.

Rnd 1: k

Rnd 2: *k2, m1, k to 2 sts from end of front sts, m1, k2, rep from * on back sts. 28 sts

Rnd 3: rep rnd 2. 32 sts

Rnds 4-11: rep rnds 1-2 4 times. 48 sts

Rnds 12-21: k 10 rnds.

Rnd 22: *k1, ssk, k to 3 sts from end of front sts, k2tog, k1, rep from * on back sts. 44 sts

Rnds 23-25: k 3 rnds.

Rnd 26: rep rnd 22. 40 sts

Rnd 27: k.

Rnds 28-31: rep rnds 26-27 twice. 32 sts

Rnds 32-35: rep rnd 22 4 times. 16 sts.

Rnds 36-40: k 5 rnds.

Shoulders

Rnd 41: k1, pm, k5, pm, k3, pm, k5, pm, k2

Rnd 42: *k to marker, m1, slm, k1, m1, rep from * 3 times, k to end. 24 sts.

Rnd 43: k

Rnds 44-53: rep rnds 42-43 5 times ending last rnd at final marker. 64 sts.

Rnd 54: remove marker, k1, sl next 14 sts onto scrap yarn, remove marker, cast on 2 sts, k to next marker, remove marker, k1, sl next 14 sts onto scrap yarn, cast on 2 sts, k 19. This is the new beginning of the rnd. Divide sts so that the 20 front sts are on 1 needle and the 20 back sts are on the 2nd or divided evenly over 2 needles.

Body

K 20 rnds even.

Next rnd: k10, sl next 20 sts onto scrap yarn, k10.

Legs

The first leg will be worked on the 20 sts on the needles. Divide sts so that the 10 front sts are on 1 needle and the 10 back sts are on the 2nd or divided evenly over 2 needles.

K 40 rnds even.

Switch to shoe yarn and k 9 rnds.

Next rnd: k1, ssk, k4, k2tog, k2, ssk, k4, k2tog, k1. 16 sts.

Next rnd: k.

Next rnd: k1, ssk, k2, k2tog, k2, ssk, k2, k2tog, k1. 12 sts.

Stuff leg and kitchener stitch the front sts to the back. Return held sts for other leg to needles and work as for first.

Arms

Return held sts for one arm to needles. Pick up and knit 2 sts from cast on sts at underarm. Divide the 16 sts so that these 2 sts are the first and last sts of the rnd.

K 26 rnds even.

Next rnd: k1, ssk, k2, k2tog, k2, ssk, k2, k2tog, k1. 12 sts.

Next rnd: k.

Next rnd: k1, ssk, k2tog, k2, ssk, k2tog, k1. 8 sts.

Stuff arm and kitchener stitch the front sts to the back.

Work 2nd arm in the same way.

Finishing

Use ends to stitch closed any holes at the underarms and crotch and bury all ends on the inside. Using body colour duplicate stitch detail on the shoes as shown in photo.

Embroider features using hair colour (or dark yarn) working french knots for the eyes and backstitch for the mouth. Don't be afraid to re-work the features until you get an expression you're happy with!

Hair

Cut a piece of cardboard approx 5" / 12.5cm wide (or about 1" / 2.5cm wider than desired hair length). Wrap hair yarn around cardboard for approx 3" / 7.5cm, wrapping 4 layers.

Without removing yarn from card create parting by working a row of backstitch across wrapped yarn, being careful to stitch through all layers. Remove card and cut across loop directly opposite parting. Sew hair to head by backstitching over previous stitching. Use dress yarn to stitch 'barrettes' on either side of the parting. Trim hair as necessary.

Dress

Working with 2 needles cast on 8 sts in dress yarn. The bib of the dress is worked back and forth in garter st.

Row 1: k.

Row 2: k2, yo, k4, yo, k2. 10 sts.

Row 3: k.

Row 4: k2, m1, k to 2 sts from end, m1, k2. 12 sts.

Rows 5-10: rep rows 3-4 3 more times. 18 sts.

Row 11: k. Without breaking yarn cast on 22 sts next to sts just worked. 40 sts total.

Divide sts evenly over 2 needle tips or 3 dpns and join rnd.

Next rnd: p.

Next rnd: k.

Repeat last 2 rnds once.

Next rnd: (k2, m1) to end. 60 sts.

K 30 rnds even. Work 6 rnds in garter st. Bind off.

Straps

Working with 2 dpns cast on 20 sts. K 1 row. Bind off. Repeat for 2nd strap. Sew straps to top centre back of dress and sew buttons to other ends of straps. Buttons could be a choking hazard on a doll for a young child, in that case you can just stitch the straps down and embroider 'buttons' if desired. Weave in ends.

Cairn

Stay cosy in this stylish and practical beanie and fingerless mitts set worked in two colours. The interesting textured stitch pattern helps to keep you warm and is simply achieved with slip stitches - meaning that you're only ever working with a single colour per round. The hat is given in four sizes, and the mitts in three so you can be sure of a perfect fit.

Materials

Yarn - Mitts: 37[47, 56] yds / 34[43, 51]m of colour A; 48[60, 72] yds / 44[55, 66]m of colour B; **Hat:** 60[72, 88, 94] yds / 55[66, 80, 86]m of colour A and 36[43, 57, 61] yds / 33[39, 52, 56]m of colour B of double knitting / light worsted weight yarn. Shown in Devon Fine Fibres Bowmont DK (100% bowmont braf wool, 166 yds / 152m, 1.76oz /50g) in grey (A) and red (B).

Needles - 3.25 16" / 40cm circular, 4mm 16" / 40cm circular, 4mm set of 4 dpns.

Notions - 5 markers, scrap yarn.

Gauge

22 sts and 32 rnds = 4" /10cm in slipped st pattern

Note - yarn quantities given do not allow for swatching. On a small item like this I prefer to check gauge after working a few inches. Beginning with the mitts makes more sense than making a mitt sized swatch first!

Size

Hat - xs[s, m, l] to fit approx head circumference of 18[20, 22, 24]" / 46[51, 56, 61] cm

Mitts - s[m, l] to fit approx hand circumference of 6[7.5, 9]" / 15[19, 22] cm

Hat and mitts are both shown in m.

Mitts

With colour A and dpns, cast on 32[40, 48] sts, join rnd and distribute sts evenly over 3 needles.

Rnd 1: p.
Next rnd: k.
Next rnd: p.
Switch to yarn B.
Next 3 rnds: k4, (sl2, k6) to 4 sts from end, sl2, k2.
Switch to yarn A.
Next rnd: k.
Next rnd: p.
Rep last 2 rnds once.
Switch to yarn B.
Next 6 rnds: (sl2, k6) to end.
Switch to yarn A.
Next rnd: k.
Next rnd: p.
Rep last 2 rnds once.
Switch to yarn B.

Next 3 rnds: k4, (sl2, k6) to 4 sts from end, sl2, k2.

Next rnd - right mitt: k4, sl2, k1, k4 with scrap yarn, slip 4 sts just knit back to left needle, pick up yarn B, k5, (sl2, k6) to 2 sts from end, k2.

Next rnd - left mitt: k4, (sl2, k6) to 9 sts from end, k4 with scrap yarn, slip 4 sts just knit back to left needle, pick up yarn B, k5, sl2, k2.

Next 2 rnds: k4, (sl2, k6) to 4 sts from end, sl2, k2.
*Switch to yarn A.
Next rnd: k.
Next rnd: p.
Rep last 2 rnds once.
Switch to yarn B.
Next 6 rnds: (sl2, k6) to end.

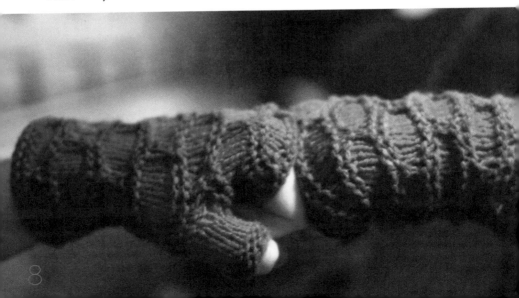

Switch to yarn A.
Next rnd: k.
Next rnd: p.
Rep last 2 rnds once.
Switch to yarn B.*
Next 6 rnds: k4, (sl2, k6) to 4 sts from end, sl2, k2.
Rep from * to * once more.
Next 3 rnds: k4, (sl2, k6) to 4 sts from end, sl2, k2.
Switch to yarn A.
Next rnd: k.
Next rnd: p.
Bind off.

Thumb

Carefully remove scrap yarn and slip 4 held sts on each side onto dpns. With yarn B *k across 4 sts on one needle, pick up and knit 1[2, 3] sts between needles, rep from *. 10[12, 14] sts.
Distribute sts evenly over 3 dpns and k 4 rnds.
Switch to yarn A.
Next rnd: k.
Next rnd: p.

Finishing

Weave in ends closing up any holes at base of thumb.

Hat

With smaller circular and colour A, cast on 88[104, 112, 120] sts, join rnd, placing marker to mark beg of rnd.

> **Optional** - a tubular cast on for 2x2 rib can be used for a neat edge, there is a video tutorial at - http://ysolda.com/pictorial-guides/

Rnd 1: (k2, p2) to end.
Rnds 2-16: rep rnd 1 15 times.
Switch to larger circular and yarn B.

Sizes xs and s only -
Next 3 rnds: k4, (sl2, k6) to 4 sts from end, sl2, k2.

Sizes m and l only -
Next 3 rnds: (sl2, k6) to end.
Switch to yarn A.
Next rnd: k.
Next rnd: p.
Rep last 2 rnds once.
Switch to yarn B.
Next 6 rnds: k4, (sl2, k6) to 4 sts from end, sl2, k2.

All sizes -
Switch to yarn A.
Next rnd: k.
Next rnd: p.
Rep last 2 rnds once.
Switch to yarn B.

Next 6 rnds: (sl2, k6) to end.
Switch to yarn A.
Next rnd: k.
Next rnd: p.
Rep last 2 rnds once.
Switch to yarn B.
Next 6 rnds: k4, (sl2, k6) to 4 sts from end, sl2, k2.
Switch to yarn A.
Next rnd: (k6, k2tog) to end. 77[91, 98, 105] sts.
Next rnd: p.
Next rnd: k.
Next rnd: p.
Switch to yarn B.
Next 5 rnds: (sl2, k5) to end.
Switch to yarn A and distribute sts evenly on dpns.
Next rnd: (k5, k2tog) to end. 66[78, 84, 90] sts.
Next rnd: p.
Next rnd: k.
Next rnd: p.
Switch to yarn B.
Next 4 rnds: k3, (sl2, k4) to 3 sts from end, sl2, k1.
Switch to yarn A.
Next rnd: (k4, k2tog) to end. 55[65, 70, 75] sts.
Next rnd: p.
Next rnd: k.
Next rnd: p.
Switch to yarn B.
Next 3 rnds: (sl2, k3) to end.
Switch to yarn A.

Next rnd: (k9[11, 12, 13], k2tog, pm) to end. 50[60, 65, 70] sts.
Next rnd: (p to 2 sts before marker, p2tog) to end. 45[50, 60, 65] sts.
Next rnd: (k to 2 sts before marker, k2tog) to end. 40[50, 55, 60] sts.
Rep last 2 rnds until 10 sts remain.

Finishing
Break yarn and draw through remaining sts. Weave in ends.

> **Tip** - try using a balloon as a hat form to block the hat over. Inflate the balloon to slightly less than the head circumference of the wearer (to avoid stretching the hat out). Shape the hat over it while damp and leave to dry. The stitch pattern used in Cairn can look rather crumpled after knitting so blocking like this helps to open it out.

Hap Blanket

Snuggle up in this pretty blanket inspired by the traditional everyday shawls of the Shetland Isles. The blanket begins with the centre square of squishy garter stitch worked in a simple stripe pattern. Then the feather and fan (old shale) edging is worked by picking up stitches around the centre square and working outwards in rounds in a stripe pattern that echoes the beautiful shading often found on hap shawls. If this simple example of the basic idea inspires you to learn more about hap shawls, Sharon Miller's *Shetland Hap Shawls Then & Now* is a wonderful reference.

Materials

Yarn - 550 yds / 500m of MC and 130 yds / 120m of CC of heavy aran / bulky weight yarn.
Shown in MC - Artesano Aran (50% alpaca / 50% wool, 144 yds / 132m, 3.53oz /100g) in Pine and CC - Manos Del Uruguay Wool Classica (100% wool, 138 yds / 126m, 3.53oz /100g) in 6422.
Needles - 8mm 32" / 80cm or longer circular needle.
Notions - 4 markers.

Gauge

11 sts and 19 rows = 4" /10cm in garter st

Size

Approx 40" / 1m square

> **Notes** - slip the first st of every row. When working CC stripes carry MC up side without breaking, but cut and re-join CC for each stripe.

Centre

With MC cast on 60 sts, k 10 rows.
*With CC k 2 rows, with MC k 20 rows; rep from * 3 times.
With CC k 2 rows, with MC k 10 rows. Bind off with MC.

Edging

With MC pick up and knit 61 sts along each side of centre square, placing markers at corners after each set of 61 sts. Join rnd, the final marker placed will mark the beginning of rnd. 244 sts.

Working either from chart or written directions work feather and fan edging. Work rnds 11-14, 23-26, and 35-36 in CC and all other rnds in MC.

Rnd 1: p.
Rnd 2: *k1, yo, k to marker, yo, slm, rep from * to end.
Rnd 3: k.
Rnd 4: *k1, yo, k1, [k2tog twice, (yo, k1) 4 times, k2tog twice] to 1 st before marker, k1, yo, slm, rep from * to end.

Rnds 5-7: rep rnds 1-3.
Rnd 8: *k1, yo, k3, [k2tog twice, (yo, k1) 4 times, k2tog twice] to 3 sts before marker, k3, yo, slm, rep from * to end.

Rnds 9-11: rep rnds 1-3.
Rnd 12: *k1, yo, k5, [k2tog twice, (yo, k1) 4 times, k2tog twice] to 5 sts before marker, k5, yo, slm, rep from * to end.

Rnds 13-15: rep rnds 1-3.
Rnd 16: *(k1, yo) 3 times, k1, k2tog twice, [k2tog twice, (yo, k1) 4 times, k2tog twice] to 7 sts before marker, k2tog twice, yo, k1, yo, k2, yo, slm, rep from * to end.

Rnds 17-19: rep rnds 1-3.
Rnd 20: *k1, yo, k3, (yo, k1) twice, k2tog twice, [k2tog twice, (yo, k1) 4 times, k2tog twice] to 9 sts before marker, k2tog twice, yo, k1, yo, k4, yo, slm, rep from * to end.

Rnds 21-23: rep rnds 1-3.
Rnd 24: *k1, yo, k5, (yo, k1) twice, k2tog twice, [k2tog twice, (yo, k1) 4 times, k2tog twice] to 11 sts before marker, k2tog twice, yo, k1, yo, k6, yo, slm, rep from * to end.

Rnds 25-36: rep rnds 1-12.

Finishing

With CC bind off loosely: *p2 tog, sl st on right needle back to left needle, rep from * to end.

Weave in ends. Wet block, making sure centre is square and shaping edging into neat scallops.

Nap Blanket

Edging Chart

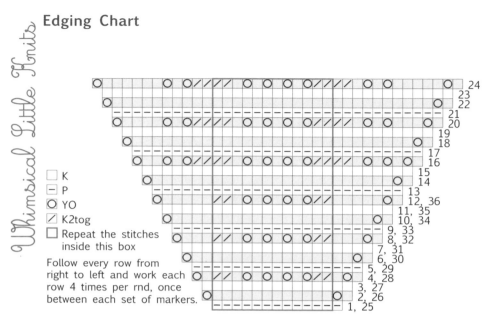

Legend:
- ☐ K
- ⊟ P
- Ⓞ YO
- ⊘ K2tog
- ☐ Repeat the stitches inside this box

Follow every row from right to left and work each row 4 times per rnd, once between each set of markers.

Row numbers (right side): 24, 23, 22, 21, 20, 19, 18, 17, 16, 15, 14, 13, 12, 36, 11, 35, 10, 34, 9, 33, 8, 32, 7, 31, 6, 30, 5, 29, 4, 28, 3, 27, 2, 26, 1, 25

Icing Swirl Hat

A cute slouchy hat that knits up quickly in a bulky yarn. Featuring just enough lace detailing to keep things interesting, without requiring too much attention. The hat begins at the top with a simple I-cord and is then joined in the round, increasing with columns of spiralling yarn overs. All of the shaping is worked at the centre back, perfectly gathering the extra slouchy fabric.

Materials

Yarn - 100yds / 90m chunky / bulky yarn. Shown in Misti Alpaca Chunky (100% alpaca, 108yds / 99m, 3.53oz / 100g) in Lipstick.
Needles - 6mm set of 4 dpns, 6mm 16" / 40cm circular needle.
Notions - 9 markers - 1 in a contrast colour / style.

> **Note** - yarn quantities given do not allow for swatching. On a small item like this I prefer to check gauge after working a few inches. If you wish to make a separate swatch this will require more yarn.

Size

s[l] to fit approx head circumference of 20" / 51cm[22" / 56cm]

Gauge

14 sts and 18 rnds = 4" /10cm in st st

Directions

Working with only 2 dpns cast on 3 sts. Work 2.5" / 7cm of i-cord - *k3, slide sts to other end of dpn without turning, rep from *.
Kfb of each stitch and then join these 6 sts in the rnd distributing 2 sts on each of 3 dpns.

Rnd 1: (k1, pm, k1) 3 times.
Rnd 2: (yo, k to marker, slm, yo, k to end of needle) 3 times. 12 sts.
Rnd 3: k to end.
Rep rnds 2 and 3 7 times. 54 sts.

Next rnd: (yo, k to marker, slm, yo, k to end of needle) 3 times. 60 sts.
Next rnd: (k all sts from dpn onto circular without removing marker, pm) 3 times. All sts should now be on the circular with a marker every 10 sts, use a contrasting marker to mark the end of the rnd.
Next rnd: (yo, k to marker, slm) 6 times.
Next rnd: k to end.
Rep last 2 rnds 2[4] times. 78[90] sts.
Next rnd: (yo, k to 2 sts before marker, k2tog, slm) 6 times.
Next rnd: k to end.
Rep last 2 rnds 6 times.
Next rnd: (yo, k to 2 sts before marker, k2tog, slm) 6 times.

Next rnd: (k to 2 sts before marker, k2tog, slm) 6 times. 72[84] sts.

Next rnd: (yo, k to 2 sts before marker, k2tog, slm) 6 times.

Next rnd: k2tog 18[21] times without removing markers, (k6[7], pm, k to marker, slm,) to end. 54[63] sts with a marker every 6[7] sts.

Next rnd: (yo, k to 2 sts before marker, k2tog, slm) 9 times.

Next rnd: k to end.

Rep last 2 rnds 2 times. Bind off.

Finishing

Weave in ends. Block, shaping over a balloon can work well to open up the yarn overs. Tie i-cord in knot.

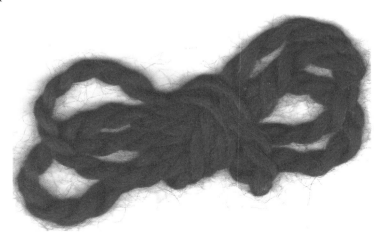

Grown Up Booties

What could be better than wrapping your feet in snug, squishy garter stitch? This is a very simple pattern that any beginner could easily tackle, while its nostalgic appeal and endless adaptability make it a fun project for even the most experienced knitter. Try embellishing your booties with ribbons, pom-poms or buttons.

Materials

Yarn - 110m / 120 yds of heavy aran / bulky weight yarn. Shown in Artesano Aran in sunset.
Needles - 5mm needles.
Notions - 2 markers.

Gauge

16 sts and 40 rows = 10cm / 4" in garter st

Sizing

Designed to fit an adult, length is adjustable.

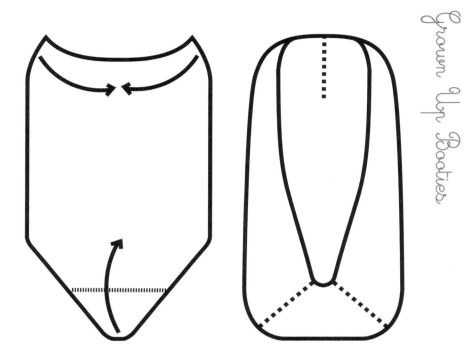

Directions

Cast on 24 sts.

Row 1: K
Row 2: k10, pm, k4, pm, k10
Row 3: k to marker, slm, kfb, k to 1 st before marker, kfb, slm, k to end.
Rep row 3 4 more times. 34 sts, 14 between markers.

Remove markers and knit even until the un-stretched work is approx 5cm / 2" shorter than the length of the foot.

Next row: k1, k2tog, k to 3 sts from end, k2tog, k1.
Next row: k to end.
Rep last 2 rows until 6 sts remain.

Next row: k1, k2tog, k2tog, k1.
Next row: k2tog twice.
Bind off remaining 2 sts.

Finishing

Fold cast on edge in half and seam to make heel. Fold point up to beginning of decreases and seam along each diagonal edge to form toe. Fold and seam lines are shown in illustration.

For more patterns by Ysolda
visit www.ysolda.com